Tu

SPIRITUALITY

for CHRISTIANS

Compiled by
Stephen Joseph Wolf

idjc press

Dedicated
to
Dr. Vernon J. Bittner,
John Behnke, C.S.P.,
and Gerald G. May, M.D.
with gratitude
for the influence of their work

Twelve Step Spirituality for Christians was originally compiled
by Rev. Steve Wolf for the *FIAT (Faith In Action Together) Groups*
of St. Stephen Catholic Community in
Hermitage, Old Hickory, & Mt. Juliet,
and completed while serving as Associate Pastor at
St. Henry Church in Nashville, Tennessee.

See pages 2, 72 and 73 for other sources.

Cover photographs of Malta are by the compiler.

Printed in the U.S.A. and distributed by Ingram Books
Published by idjc press; contact at steve@idjc.info

ISBN 978-0-9795549-8-8

Additional copies are available from
St. Mary's Bookstore in Nashville, Tennessee
www.stmarysbookstore.com
www.amazon.com
and other fine bookstores.

PRAYER FOR A CULTURE OF ADDICTION

God of mercy,
we bless you in the name of your Son,
who ministered to all who came to him.

Give your strength to your servants
who are bound by the chains of addiction.

Enfold them in your love
and restore them to
the freedom of God's children.

Lord, look with compassion
on all your sons and daughters
who have lost their health and freedom.

Restore to them
the assurance of your unfailing mercy,
and strengthen them in the work of recovery.

To those who care for them,
grant patient understanding
and a love that perseveres.

We ask this through Christ our Lord.
Amen.

POSSIBLE GROUP GROUND RULES

Faith Sharing is:

Regular: I will do my best to make all sessions.

Voluntary: No one is required to share. The tone is invitational. Verbal participation is encouraged but not demanded.

Not Interrupted: When someone is sharing, everyone listens before commenting or speaking. Side conversations are avoided; one person at a time.

Not Contradicted: The sharing is based on the person's own life story, so conclusions or critiques of what is shared are not appropriate. Avoid trying to take away feelings with comments like, *You shouldn't feel that way.*

Done In "I" Language: beginning with *I think* or *I feel* rather than *Mary said* or *Joe thinks.*

Confidential: What is said in the group stays in the group.

(These ground rules are drawn from Joye Gros' *Theological Reflection,* Loyola Press, 2002. Groups are free to alter them as they wish.)

I agree with the group ground rules.   (Signature and Date)

Twelve Step Spirituality for Christians

Members of **faith sharing groups** are encouraged to bring their favorite Bible to weekly meetings; follow the opening passages in your Bible as you hear them read.

If you read this book **on your own**, you will get much more from it by beginning each chapter with the short passages indicated from your own Bible.

A.A. Disclaimer

The Twelve Steps and Twelve Traditions of Alcoholics Anonymous have been reprinted in their original form, and have been loosely adapted in this compilation.

Permission to reprint and adapt the Twelve Steps and Twelve Traditions of Alcoholics Anonymous does not mean that Alcoholics Anonymous is in any way affiliated, nor that it has read and/or endorses the contents of this publication, nor that A.A. agrees with the views expressed herein.

A.A. is a program of recovery from alcoholism only - inclusion of the Steps in this publication, or use in any other non-A.A. context, does not imply otherwise. Additionally, while A.A. is a spiritual program, A.A. is not a religious program. Thus, A.A. is not affiliated or allied with any sect, denomination, or specific religious belief.

Editor's Disclaimer

The main goal of this little book is to expose twelve step spirituality to Christians who may not be familiar with it. Behind this is a conviction that ours is a culture of addiction, called to be a culture of life and a culture of vocation. Psychiatrist Gerald May, MD, says it well:

I have come to view addiction as the sacred disease of the modern world. Addictions can be tragedies, but on occasion they can be gifts as well. At rock bottom, one is forced either to reach out toward the wonderful mystery of life or continue with a willfulness that will obviously end in death. It will help to remember that we are all addicts.
(*Will and Spirit*, May, pg. 41)

I make no claim to be an expert in the twelve steps. As a fan and admiring outsider, I have seen God's grace work through the gut-wrenching honesty and trust in God that are required of patient workers of the steps. If you want to meet the core of humanity, talk to an alcoholic in recovery.

My first exposure to addiction and the twelve steps was through members of my large extended family. I can still see my grandmother pointing at my brothers and me as we drank a cold beer at a family gathering declaring, "just remember: it's in your blood!" Indeed, addiction is in our blood, our family history.

I remember too telling a seminary classmate in the program that I did not really understand addiction until the day it hit me that if I were told that I could never again eat even one cookie… It may seem rude to equate the damage of cookies with the havoc wrought by demon rum. Let me just say that total abstinence from cookies strikes me as simply impossible. My seminary friend understood, and his response was honest and hilarious: "We name it 'cookie'! Cunning! Baffling! Powerful!"

3

As a parish priest and spiritual director, I regularly encounter diverse evidence of the addictive nature of our culture. Seeking to let God grow me into the particular human God has created me to be, regular review of the twelve steps in personal prayer has proven invaluable. In moving to health against a drift of depression, the simple HALT question (hungry?, angry?, lonely?, tired?) has been a real lifesaver. Some familiarity with these twelve steps will most certainly enrich the life and prayer of every woman or man on any faith journey.

Friends in recovery have advised that the best treatment program for addiction begins with 90 meetings in 90 days. They also wisely caution to accept and not lose heart on those days we may take one step forward and two steps back. What a help has been the truth of how often that compelling urge will pass while calling a friend or going to prayer for ten minutes or, sometimes, for ten seconds.

Countless heroes in recovery give witness that they wanted there to be (and searched without success for) an easier or different way than the twelve steps. A.A. gives witness to us all of the call of our Maker to honesty, fidelity, freedom and openness to the wholly unmerited grace of God.

- Stephen Joseph Wolf

Twelve Steps In Six Weeks?

To "mess with" the twelve steps is a risky business. For that reason, please keep in mind throughout these six weeks that each of the twelve steps is necessary on its own. Indeed, this book is not the program; it is offered for awareness of its spirituality.

So, (not to excuse running through the twelve steps in six weeks, but) Bill W.'s first draft had six steps:

1   We admitted that we were licked, that we were powerless over alcohol.

2   We made a moral inventory of our defects or sins.

3   We confessed and shared our shortcomings with another person in confidence.

4   We made restitution to all those we had harmed by our drinking.

5   We tried to help other alcoholics, with no thought of reward in money or prestige.

6   We prayed to whatever God we thought there was for power to practice these precepts. ("Pass It On", page 197)

Let us keep this in mind: The lessons learned by A.A. in the experience of working the steps led them to expand these six into what is now known as the twelve.

First Step Prayer

Today,
I ask for help with my addiction.
Denial has kept me from seeing
how powerless I am
and how my life is unmanageable.
I need to learn and remember
that I have an incurable illness
and that abstinence is
the only way to deal with it.

The Twelve Step Prayer Book,, page 67

1

When I Am Weak...

1ˢᵗ
step

We admit our need for God's gift of salvation, that we are powerless over certain areas of our lives and that our lives are at times sinful and unmanageable. _(Bittner)

One member of the group reads: **Romans 7:15-25**
as other members read silently.

2ⁿᵈ member of the group reads: **John 5:1-18**
as other members read silently.

Take turns reading the following background reflections from 90 Days, One Day At A Time, by John Behnke, C.S.P. (Paulist Press, 1999).

Our disease is cunning and baffling. It's hard to get a handle on it. We want it cured once and for all. But just when we think we have it under control and we understand the ins and outs of the problem, it rears its ugly head... Sometimes it sneaks its way in through a back door disguised and thinly veiled in new forms and shapes.

In recovery, our disease is often described as a sleeping tiger. A wild, untamed, crafty, unpredictable animal who is resting, gaining strength, plotting and planning for the next violent assault on our sober and clean recovery...

For the most part, our real line of defense is gathering together in a fellowship of strength with others susceptible to the periodic onslaughts of possible relapse.
(John Behnke, C.S.P., day 22)

During the first weeks of recovery it was difficult to accept the fact that I was an alcoholic. It seemed like a shameful lack of moral fiber that stigmatized me.

One day I was in the doctor's office getting some sort of checkup. The doctor had a soft-spoken, kindly way about him. He may have detected my apprehension during this procedure. Reassuringly he said to me, "You know you've got a disease. It's alcoholism. It's not your fault that you have this disease. But now that you know you've got it, you've got a responsibility to do something about it."

Those soft-spoken words made all the difference.

It's a disease, not a moral problem. And the nice thing about this disease is that I don't have to take pills for the rest of my life to counteract it. I just don't need to put any type of mind-altering substances in my body.

I'm glad I'm an alcoholic. (day 35)

I have a friend who has been around the program longer than I. He comes in, surrenders, stays around for a few months and then goes back out. "I know what I have to do," he tells me. And he does. He's got the jargon down cold. He even throws in a lot of stuff about how his Higher Power is in his life.

Every time he disappears, I want to search him out and shake some sense into him, because I know what's best for him. I want to save him because I see what great potential he has. I know what he has to do, and I want to make him do it for his own good.

The program has taught me that I can't fix everything and everyone. The only one I can do anything about is myself. I need to be single-minded in my own recovery program and not allow extraneous frustrations and disappointments to get in the way of my own sobriety. I can be there, but I can't save. I don't like that, but that's the way real life is played out. Part of my program is to accept the way things are - the things I have no control over. (day 26)

There are lots of things I am grateful for in my life. The program itself is pure gift. It has enabled me to have close contact with my Higher Power. I have been given my life back, sober and clean, with all the wonderful opportunities it offers me on a daily basis.

If I were to single out one thing I was particularly grateful about, it would be the fact that I am an alcoholic. I have been called a lot of things in my life, some good, some bad. I have, from earliest recollection, felt out of step, out of sync, with the rest of the world. The term *alcoholic* seems to fit like an old comfortable shoe. It answers a lot of the questions and fills in a lot of the gaps. Finally I know why my crazy past was just that - crazy. I am an alcoholic, plain and simple. It all finally makes sense. It doesn't solve the problems, but it at least points me in the right direction.

On a daily basis, I can do something about the problem by not picking up, working the steps, staying close to the fellowship and praying. (Behnke, day 28)

*Three times I begged the Lord about this
[thorn in the flesh], that it might leave me,
but he said to me, "My grace is sufficient for you,
for power is made perfect in weakness"…
I am content with weaknesses, insults,
hardships, persecutions, and constraints,
for the sake of Christ,
for when I am weak, then I am strong.*

2 Corinthians 12:8,9a,10

Courage is fear that has said its prayers.

One Day at a Time in Al-Anon, 1985, 2000 (March 24, pg. 84)

10

REFLECTION

* from Vernon J. Bittner's *You Can Help With Your Healing*

1. What area of my life might God be calling me to bring to healing and openness to growth?

2. What obstacles might keep me from trusting this process enough to become more aware of how God works with my humanity?

3.* When, like Paul, have I had to admit my own powerlessness (Romans 7:15-21)?

4. It has been said that we live in an "addictive culture." What signs of this can I name?

5.* What feelings surface with me around the word "surrender"?

6.* In Corinthians and Ephesians, St. Paul writes of his weaknesses being turned into strengths. How can my weaknesses become strengths?

7. How could anyone be happy about being an alcoholic?

Closing Prayer:

Are there intercessions from the group?

Conclude with the Our Father, then the prayer and song on pages 74 and 75.

Second Step Prayer

I pray for an open mind
so I may come to believe
in a Power greater than myself.
I pray for humility
and the continued opportunity
to increase my faith.
I don't want to be crazy anymore.

The Twelve Step Prayer Book, page 67

A Prayer for the Third Step

Take, Lord, and receive all my liberty,
my memory, my understanding and my entire will,
all I have and call my own.
You have given all to me.
To you, Lord, I return it.
Everything is yours; do with it what you will.
Give me only your love and your grace;
that is enough for me.

St. Ignatius of Loyola

2

Let Go and Let God

2ⁿᵈ step We come to believe through the Holy Spirit that a power who came in the person of Jesus Christ, and who is greater than ourselves, can transform our weaknesses into strengths. (Bittner)

3ʳᵈ step We make a decision to turn our will and our lives over to the care of Christ as we understand him - hoping to understand him more fully. (Bittner)

One member of the group reads: **Luke 10:38-42**
as other members read silently.

2ⁿᵈ member of the group reads: **Matthew 6:25-34**
as other members read silently.

13

Take turns reading the following background reflections from 90 Days, One Day At A Time, by John Behnke, C.S.P. (Paulist Press, 1999) and from You Can Help With Your Healing, by Vernon J. Bittner (Augsburg, 1993).

In the active days of our drinking, few things in life were left unaffected by the excessive use of alcohol. Many parts of our lives fell by the wayside.

As we closed in upon ourselves, service-oriented projects were not so important any longer. They took up too much precious time. The gains and perks from those endeavors were too imperceptible to calculate. We argued that our time could be better spent and more appreciated elsewhere... (John Behnke, C.S.P., day 72)

I always loved the arts, especially museums and the symphony. I enjoyed eating out and discovering new, interesting restaurants with unique items on their menus.

I stopped going to museums because they took too long to walk through without a drink in hand. I stopped going to the symphony because the intermissions were not long enough to consume a sufficient amount of alcohol to get through the second half of the program. I remember...going to a restaurant someone else chose. I was appalled and swore never to eat there again. They had no liquor license.

I stopped seeing some of my longtime friends. They didn't seem to have the same interests as I did. In fact, it was quite boring to be around them. Either they didn't drink or couldn't keep up with the way I drank. They just weren't fun anymore… [(day 73)]

Peers - and people in general - got in the way. *If they would just leave me alone and stop prying and stop being so nosy. Didn't they realize how much work I already had to do? …Didn't they know that it was hard for me to say no? Why me? If I just had some time for myself, then, maybe when I was with people they might not be so bothersome.*

People wanted so much of us. They wanted more than we could give and still drink the way we wanted to, had to. One or the other had to go. The choice was simple and quick. [(day 74)]

Don't answer the phone. Don't return their calls. Stall them. Put them off. Make excuses. Don't show up. Forget to come. Be too busy. Be overworked. There's not enough time in the day. There are so many pressing things to do; there isn't time for personal obligations.

Put the wedge between us and our family and cut ties. Make sure the smoke screen's in place, because if they ever find out who we really are, they'll hate us and shun us. We've got to get rid of them first, before they hurt and then get rid of us. [(day 75)]

I never missed a day of work. I don't know what they're talking about. I never even took all the vacation time I was supposed to. I came in on days off. So, sometimes I came in a little groggy. So, sometimes I forgot appointments and didn't get assignments in on time or just under the wire. So, sometimes my clothes didn't always match, or I wore the same ones all week. So what if I took off a little early or had a two-martini lunch? I was there, wasn't I?

They say that usually the last thing to go in this progressive disease that we have is our job. It keeps the pretense up. *(Alcoholics are lazy bums who don't have jobs.)* It helps us to feign self-worth. (We are *somebody* if we have a job. We pay taxes, don't we?) But, probably the best reason to keep a job as long as we can is that it buys the booze. ^(John Behnke, C.S.P., day 76)

Figuratively, if not really, we kick and scream and fight until, with a sense of resignation, we are able to say, "Yes, I am an alcoholic. I have a disease."

Acknowledgement is a step fraught with setbacks and denials: *I may have a disease, but I can handle it. I'll try something new. I won't... It goes on and on, until I honestly acknowledge I have a disease and there is nothing I can do by myself to control it.*

God, I am an alcoholic. I am so grateful to know what all that craziness in my life stemmed from... ^(day 77)

I often thought that there wasn't anything I couldn't do if I put my mind to it. Drink brought me to my knees. I discovered that by myself I was weak and vulnerable. I had no strength, no power over the demon alcohol and its cousin, drugs.

I had to surrender and hand my life over to a power far greater than myself to find the strength within to keep the disease of alcoholism in abeyance. It's amazing that when we totally hand over our lives in a leap of faith, we get it back with the strength and wisdom and power of a loving God so that we can do, with energy to spare, what, alone, we were never able to achieve. My strength comes from my Higher Power on a daily basis, when I hand my life over to his care. [day 62]

S.L.I.P. (sobriety lost its priority)

Not often, but sometimes, my brain tells me that I'm all right. It tells me that I've been at it long enough and now I really could go out and have "a" drink. It doesn't tell me to get drunk - just to have one drink.

I need to go to meetings frequently so that I can hear firsthand from people who have been out there recently. I need to be reminded that it's not any different. I need to be reminded that one drink is never enough and a thousand is always too little.

Going to meetings isn't a guarantee that I won't relapse, but it is some insurance. It is a buffer zone between me and that first drink. Everyone who has ever come back from a relapse has indicated that before the relapse happened, they stopped going to meetings and working their program. That's more than enough proof for me. I don't want to slip (Sobriety Lost Its Priority).

I think I'll keep going to meetings. [day 66]

Healing is a fascinating word. Often we think of it in terms of cure. However, there is no such thing as a cure for the human condition or the human dilemma. Each of us will eventually die. Therefore when we think of healing, we need to think of it in terms of the Judeo-Christian tradition, which equates it with salvation, or being made whole. Being made whole or finding salvation, however, does not only pertain to our spiritual life, but to our emotional and physical life as well. It is concerned with the recovery of the proper balance of our body, mind, and spirit. (Vernon J. Bittner, pg. 9)

We pray one of two ways:

> *God, I want to be healed,*
> *But I want it to happen on my terms.*

> *God, I want to be healed,*
> *But I don't want to admit*
> *that I'm out of control.*

> *God, I want to be healed,*
> *But I want to manage my own life.*

> *God, I want to be healed,*
> *But I don't want to accept the*
> *limitations of my humanity.*

Or we accept our sickness and pray:

God, I want to be healed.

> *Help me to accept*
> > *my powerlessness,*
> > *my unmanageability,*
> > *my isolation, and*
> > *my humanity,*
> *So that healing can begin.*

God, let it begin with me now!

Let me say,
> *"Lord, I want to be healed!"*

(Vernon J. Bittner, pg. 24)

Now to him who is able to accomplish
far more than all we ask or imagine,
by the power at work within us,
to him be glory in the church
and in Christ Jesus
to all generations,
forever and ever.
Amen.

Ephesians 3:20-21

The beginning of love
is to let those we love
be perfectly themselves,
and not to twist them
to fit our own image.
Otherwise we love only
the reflection of ourselves
we find in them.
Can this be charity?

Thomas Merton, *No Man Is An Island,* and
One Day at a Time in Al-Anon, 1985 (June 13, pg. 165)

REFLECTION

* from Vernon J. Bittner's *You Can Help With Your Healing*

1.* How would I describe the role of the Holy Spirit in the journey of faith?

2.* Who is Jesus Christ to me? How do I describe my relationship with him?

3.* How do I experience the tension between being and doing; prayer and service; relation to God and loving my neighbor?

4. When and how have I attempted to be my own God?

5.* What meaning does "Seek first the kingdom of God" (Matthew 6:33) have for me?

6.* How do I react to the invitation of Jesus that God's will is for me to have life more abundantly (See John 10:10b)?

7.* What prevents me from turning my life and my will over to God's care? When I do turn my life over to Christ, what causes me to take it back at times?

Closing Prayer: Are there intercessions from the group?

Conclude with the Our Father, then the prayer and song on pages 74 and 75.

Fourth Step Prayer

Dear God,
it is I who have made my life a mess.
I have done it, but I cannot undo it.
My mistakes are mine, and I will begin
a searching and fearless moral inventory.
I will write down my wrongs,
but I will also include that which is good.
I pray for the strength
to complete the task.

Fifth Step Prayer

Higher Power,
my inventory has shown me who I am,
yet I ask for your help in admitting my wrongs
to another person and to you.
Assure me, and be with me, in this Step,
for without this Step
I cannot progress in my recovery.
With your help, I can do this, and I will do it.

The Twelve Step Prayer Book, page 68

3

Sick As Our Secrets

4th step We make a searching and fearless moral inventory of ourselves - both our strengths and our weaknesses.
(Bittner)

5th step We admit to Christ, to ourselves, and to another human being the exact nature of our sins.
(Bittner)

One member of the group reads: **Mark 12:28-34**
as other members read silently.

2nd member of the group reads: **2 Corinthians 5:16-21**
as other members read silently.

Take turns reading the following background reflections from 90 Days, One Day At A Time, by John Behnke, C.S.P. (Paulist Press, 1999) and from the Saint Meinrad Prayer Book, Saint Meinrad Alumni Association (Abbey Press, 1995).

23

It wasn't my fault. They made me do it. He talked me into it. I never had a chance. It was my circumstances that were against me. No one gave me a chance. The odds were always against me. My genes weren't the right mix. My family was never supportive. No one really understood the troubles I had. I never had a break. They were always picking on me. I never got a fair shake. If only things had been different. If only someone believed in me.

Since joining A.A. I have discovered that whenever I point the finger there are always three other fingers pointing back in my direction. (John Behnke, C.S.P., day 31)

They say we are as healthy as our deepest resentment. They tell us that holding onto resentments is the quickest way back to using actively.

Holding on to resentments sure does cause a lot of havoc and upheaval in my life. When I hold on to a resentment it festers and foments and consumes a lot of the time and energy that I could be using for more productive purposes.

When I look at the resentments I've had and have, I find they usually eat away at my insides and ruin my day, and sometimes even weeks on end. They seldom have an effect on the people I'm having such hateful thoughts about. Oftentimes they don't even have a clue about the vicious thoughts I'm harboring for them, and if they did know, it probably would cause them to lose little, if any sleep.

Resentments are a form of self-indulgence. I spend an inordinate amount of time licking my exaggerated wounds and feeling sorry for myself. They cause me to live in a fantasy rather than the here and now, doing what I really should be doing - changing and growing rather than reverting to infantile overreactions. [(day 41)]

Why do today what you can put off till tomorrow? A motto all of us alcoholics could have had hanging on our walls… Sometimes we didn't even have the energy to eat food because we had something more important to do: drink. The work, the obligations, the promises, even taking a bath were put off until tomorrow, so pressing and time-consuming was our relationship with the almighty bottle.

In most cases, tomorrow never came.

The program works if we don't pick up and use. We can get things done when they need to be done and have time left over, if we let our Higher Power be our motivating force and not let our disease consume us. [(day 65)]

1. *No one is going to tell me what to do. I don't care who they are, they don't have the right to even think they know better than I what should be done. I've had it up to here with people trying to foist their will on me. I don't have to put up with this.*

2. *I know what's best. I've put my heart and soul into this. I didn't end up in this position for nothing; when I say something, I want it followed. If it isn't done my way, I can take my ball back and go home.*

Two scenarios, one same person - a drunk, dry or sober. [(day 47)]

25

I was afraid of what they would say. I was afraid of what they were thinking. I was afraid of what they might do. I was afraid of the things I did and might do. I was afraid to try something new. I was afraid of failing, of being ridiculed, of not being understood. I was afraid of the past catching up and what the future might bring. I was afraid of being alone. I was afraid of being in a group. I was afraid of standing out in a crowd. I was afraid of never being noticed or recognized. I was afraid of going crazy. I was afraid of going to bed and missing something. I was afraid of getting out of bed. I was afraid to finish a project. I was afraid I would never finish a project. I was in fear all the time.

They say that fear is false evidence appearing real. Thank God that, in recovery, I can put one foot in front of the other and face whatever it is that I have to face today. (Behnke, day 71)

Therefore,
confess your sins to one another
and pray for one another,
that you may be healed.

James 5:16a

CONDUCTING A PERSONAL INVENTORY

From the *Saint Meinrad Prayer Book*

(This information is an adapted excerpt of the "Fourth Step Inventory" of A.A. as presented in the book *A Guide to the Fourth Step* [Hazelden Foundation, 1990]. The material that follows can also be used as an examination of conscience.)

An examination of conscience can take many forms - from a brief look over the day before retiring at night, to a more personal review of life in preparation for the Sacrament of Reconciliation, to a complete personal inventory.

Whatever our situation or circumstance, we are called to accountability. As members of the Body of Christ, we have responsibilities and obligations to our God, to one another, to the Community of Faith, and to our personal integrity.

Through human weakness, we are not always faithful to our responsibilities and obligations. Through sin, we create division among the Body of Christ.

Sin involves attitudes as well as acts - single occasions, isolated incidents, habitual events and recurring episodes. So we step back and reflect.

We entrust ourselves to the mercy of God and open ourselves to the transforming power of God's grace.

In making a personal inventory, we need to examine ourselves in as many ways as possible:

attitudes and responsibilities

- to God
- to myself
- to my family
- to my work
- to my friends
- to my neighbors
- to my community

assets

When an alcoholic wishes to make a "Step 4" in A.A., he or she looks for both assets and defects. No matter who I am, this process can work as well for me. It begins with acknowledging my assets. I need to write as many assets as I can possibly attribute to myself. Some could be:

- knowing right from wrong;
- being a good-hearted person who likes people;
- wanting to do the right thing;
- calling myself on any wrongs or failures;
- willingness to undertake a self-examination.

I can enlarge this list as I become more open with myself and my attributes.

defects

The same process must be done for my defects. Some might be:

- selfishness
- alibis
- phoneyness
- pride
- resentment
- intolerance

- impatience
- envy
- dishonest thinking
- procrastination
- self-pity
- fear

cardinal sins

pride, avarice, lust, envy, anger, gluttony, sloth

corporal works of mercy

feed the hungry, give drink to the thirsty,
clothe the naked, visit and ransom captives,
give shelter to the homeless, visit the sick,
bury the dead

spiritual works of mercy

admonish sinners, instruct the ignorant,
counsel the doubtful, comfort the sorrowful,
bear wrongs patiently, forgive all injuries,
pray for the living and the dead

the ten commandments

1 I am the Lord, your God, you shall not have any gods before me.

2 You shall not take the name of the Lord, your God, in vain.

3 Remember to keep holy the Sabbath Day.

4 Honor your father and your mother.

5 You shall not kill.

6 You shall not commit adultery.

7 You shall not steal.

8 You shall not bear false witness against your neighbor.

9 You shall not covet your neighbor's spouse.

10 You shall not covet your neighbor's goods.

divine virtues

faith, hope, love

little virtues

courtesy, cheerfulness, order, loyalty,
use of time, punctuality, sincerity,
caution in speech, kindness, patience,
tolerance, integrity, balance, gratitude

REFLECTION

* from Vernon J. Bittner's *You Can Help With Your Healing*

1.* If I resolve to make a list of my assets and defects on a separate sheet of paper, which are more difficult for me to share?

2.* How can my character traits become assets? How can they become defects?

3.* What do I hold on to that prevents my growth as a Christian?

4.* What do I value in my life? What seems to take the major part of my time and energy?

5.* How does it feel to let others know my weaknesses as well as my strengths? Why?

6.* How do I feel when I hear the words "sinner" or "broken"?

7.* What is most challenging about Confession? How has Reconciliation been helpful for me?

Closing Prayer: Are there intercessions from the group?

Conclude with the Our Father, then the prayer and song on pages 74 and 75.

Sixth Step Prayer

Dear God, I am ready for your help
in removing from me the defects of character
which I now realize are obstacles to my recovery.
Help me to continue being honest with myself,
and guide me toward spiritual and mental health.

The Twelve Step Prayer Book, page 69

A Prayer for the Seventh Step
An Act of Contrition

O my God, I am heartily sorry for my sins
and I detest my thoughts and deeds contrary to
my vocation and your complete love for me,
most of all because they offend you,
whom I do love above all things.
I firmly resolve, with the help of your grace,
to do my best, with the help of your grace,
to avoid even the near occasion of sin,
which I can do only with the help of your grace.

4

Progress, Not Perfection

6ᵗʰ step   We become entirely ready
to have Christ heal all of these
defects of character that
prevent us from having a
more spiritual lifestyle.   (Bittner)

7ᵗʰ step   We humbly ask Christ to transform
all of our shortcomings.
(Bittner)

One member of the group reads: **Psalm 51:1-14**
as other members read silently.

2ⁿᵈ member of the group reads: **Mark 5:1-20**
as other members read silently.

Take turns reading the following background reflections from 90 Days, One Day At A Time, by John Behnke, C.S.P. (Paulist Press, 1999).

I've taken my share of science and psychology courses to better understand the functions of both the body and the psyche. I've read many of the popular self-help books churned out to help us put balance in our lives.

And yet, at an A.A. meeting the poignant and right-to-the-point messages come not from polished discourses of lettered people but from meek voices softly speaking from their hearts about the experiences they've had in their lives. (John Behnke, C.S.P., day 61)

denial

Denial isn't a river in Egypt. A dear friend gave me a poster with that saying on it. I had it framed and it hangs over my desk. It's a good reminder, because sometimes I forget.

It wasn't me. I didn't do it. I can hold my liquor. I don't have a problem. If only everybody would just leave me alone. I can handle this by myself. I don't need any help. You're just picking on me. You're out to get me. You're just jealous. You need to stay out of my business.

Sometimes I forget. That's why I need to frequent my meetings to get a reality check. (day 67)

anger

At some point in our disease we become angry. We're angry with the world, angry with almost everybody in it, and even angry with ourselves.

Why is this happening to me? I don't deserve this kind of treatment. Why me? We're angry about our upbringing, angry about our parents, angry about our schooling, angry with the government, angry with the authorities. Name it and we will find fault with it. We're even angry that we drink and can't stop, though we never admit that openly.

It's so wonderful to be in recovery and to realize that I don't have to strike out at everyone and everything. Life may not be fair, but that Higher Power of mine gives me everything I need to deal with whatever will come my way today. I may not like all the results that are dished out to me, but I will be able to live through the day without using. (day 68)

bargaining

At some point in our active drinking, we sense there is something going on, that maybe we are drinking just a little too much. We can handle it though. We switch drinks. We only drink in the afternoon and at night. We promise never to get drunk like that again if only God helps us through this one. We swear that we've learned our lesson. We'll never do that again. Trust us. All we need is one more chance, please. We can lick this. Let us try it on our own. (day 69

35

depression

When all that convoluted bargaining doesn't work, we become depressed. Nothing works. Nothing goes right in our life. There's no end to the misery. There's no way out. Is that all there is to life? We can't think straight. We can't work. We can't eat. We can't enjoy anything. We can't even get out of bed. Nothing has value. Even our drinking, once the elixir of life, offers no lasting solace. (Behnke, day 70)

acceptance

There was no sense ignoring it or hoping it would go away or denying that it really was a problem. There came a point where, in order to reclaim some semblance of sanity in my life, I had to accept the fact that I am an alcoholic and will be for the rest of my life. I accept the fact that at some point in the almost forgotten past, I had crossed over that thin line between being a heavy social drinker and being an alcoholic. I accept the fact that there is no magic pill to cure me of this disease. There is no way to jump back across that line of demarcation. I am what I am. (day 78)

Sobriety came to me through a direct intervention by people who loved me and were concerned about me more than I was about myself. In fact, I had long before reconciled myself to the fact that I would drink myself to death.

While I was in a lengthy recovery/treatment program at an in-patient center, a good friend and drinking partner convinced herself that upon my immediate reentry into society, I would whisk her off to an A.A. meeting and thus save her from her own pain- and suffering-filled life... Actually a good month passed and I never once suggested or demanded that she follow me to a meeting... One morning around 3 A.M., she reached bottom and phoned...

In our own time. At our own pace. The program works only for those who want it, and not for all who need it. (day 24)

For many years of my active addiction, only the most formal prayers of my faith could be recited. Any thought of a personalized prayer to a loving God had been obliterated by the need to worship wholeheartedly the spirit within the bottle of the day. My days and my life had turned into chaos, totally disrupted by the primary need to have a drink.

What a blessing to become sober and discover a Higher Power concerned about my well-being and offering me, through the program of A.A., the opportunity to lead a life filled with (**G**) Good (**O**) Orderly (**D**) Direction. Not a vengeful, hateful, punitive God, but a God offering a way to peace and happiness with a few helpful guideposts set up to show us the way and point the direction.

I find that when I allow this God into my life and want to please him with the way I live my life, I have Good Orderly Direction. And I find the opposite to be true too. When I have Good Orderly Direction in my life, I find I then have God close by my side. And isn't that what I've always wanted? Some intimacy with the creator of the big picture. Some direction. ^(Behnke, day 32)

Sometimes it's a commercial on TV that does it. Sometimes it's an outside billboard. Sometimes it's being too close to the old, familiar people, places and things. Sometimes it's because I worked too hard, or I'm too tired, or because I feel frustrated over being between a rock and a hard place. Sometimes it's because it's a happy day, or a particularly sad day, or any of the other old excuses. Sometimes it's just because something inside tells me I can handle it now. Every once in a while I get this undying urge to take a drink. Not lots of drinks …just a drink.

Two things usually cross my mind when I'm in that pre-using mood. They are things I learned early on in recovery. First, I never had just a drink. Second, an undying urge usually lasts about ten seconds. If I use that time to stall by praying or calling another person in recovery, it will pass as quickly as it appeared.

I have to be vigilant of the triggers that, once pulled, would always result in a day, or even days, of uncontrolled, excessive drinking. [day 32]

Hungry, Angry, Lonely, Tired

I don't have them often (now), but there are some days when absolutely nothing seems to be going right no matter what I do... It is at those times that my program teaches me to stop and evaluate what's going on. H.A.L.T. Usually when I step back for a moment to review the day thus far, it happens that I'm not taking care of myself... Most of those times I'm either hungry, angry, lonely, or tired... God, why didn't I think of that simple stuff before? Thank you. [day 39]

Barney Fife: *Otis, you need a hobby!*
Otis Campbell: *I* have *a hobby. Drinking!*
The Andy Griffith Show

39

Ask and it will be given to you;
seek and you will find;
knock and the door will be opened for you.
For everyone who asks, receives;
and the one who seeks, finds;
and to the one who knocks,
the door will be opened.

Matthew 7:7-8

Most of the shadows of this life
are caused by
standing in one's own sunshine.

Ralph Waldo Emerson

REFLECTION

* from Vernon J. Bittner's *You Can Help With Your Healing*

1.* What does "entirely ready" mean for me?

2.* Letting go so that I can let God help me with my destructive behavior is a leap of faith. What might prevent me from taking that risk?

3.* What feelings does the word "change" bring?

4. How do I want my relationships to grow?

5.* What does it mean for me to "humbly ask" for something?

6.* In what ways do I isolate myself from others? From God?

7.* What could I tell others about how Christ is working in my life? How might this help them and help me?

Closing Prayer:

Are there intercessions from the group?

Conclude with the Our Father, then the prayer and song on pages 74 and 75.

Eighth Step Prayer

Higher Power, I ask your help in making my list
of all those I have harmed.
I will take responsibility for my mistakes,
and be forgiving to others
as you are forgiving to me.
Grant me the willingness to begin my restitution.
This I pray.

Ninth Step Prayer

Higher Power, I pray for
the right attitude to make my amends,
being ever mindful
not to harm others in the process.
I ask for your guidance in making indirect amends.
Most important, I will continue to make amends
by staying abstinent, helping others,
and growing in spiritual progress.

The Twelve Step Prayer Book, page 69, 70

5

Let It Begin With Me

8th   We make a list
step   of all persons we have harmed
and become willing
to make amends to them all.   (Bittner)

9th   We make direct amends
step   to such persons whenever possible,
except when to do so would injure
them or others.
  (Bittner)

One member of the group reads: **Ephesians 4:1-16**
as other members read silently.

2nd member of the group reads: **Matthew 5:21-42**
as other members read silently.

Take turns reading the following background reflections.

al-anon

The Al-Anon Family Groups have given permission to reprint some excerpts in this chapter, which does not mean that al-anon has reviewed, approved, or agrees with the content of this book. [See page 72.]

Many people who faithfully work the twelve steps are not addicts themselves, or rather, more correctly, they are not addicted to alcohol or drugs. Bill Wilson's wife, Lois, discovered assistance in healing and coping by gathering with other wives of early members of A.A., regularly sharing their experiences. They also "realized their own need for change." [Al-Anon's Twelve Steps & Twelve Traditions, Preamble] These gatherings of family members and friends of alcoholics grew into what is now known as Al-Anon Family Groups, or simply as al-anon.

The family is where the impact of an addiction is up close and personal. When a child grows up in a household with an addict, the child learns those same patterns of denial, secrecy, cover-up, and other coping mechanisms akin to walking always on eggshells. When an addiction manifests itself in violence or anger, the effects of waiting for the next outburst can be obvious. Children learn early the nature of a family secret, and a culture of addiction generates a true need for safe sharing.

In pastoral counseling, I am often surprised at how readily spouses of alcoholics and drug addicts are open to the possibility that something connected to their spouse's addiction is part of what they found attractive. Perhaps the addiction of a boyfriend or girlfriend touches that place in us all that wants to be needed, the desire to be a hero. Perhaps it was the intriguing challenge of someday "fixing" him or her. Perhaps it was a conviction that he or she will change because he or she loves me that much, or if not for love of me, then for love of our children.

One great gift of al-anon, from my vantage, has been the capacity to admit that no one can fix another, that one's role as "enabler" may have been quite unhelpful, and that the only person I can change is myself.

I owe a very precious debt of gratitude to al-anon. In my early thirties, with feet still healthy enough for jogging and a serious runner as a friend and co-worker, we began to run on our lunch break, followed with a quick lunch at his nearby apartment. One of his prayer books was *One Day at a Time in Al-Anon* [1985]. On one "June 13" we were both caught by its entry from Thomas Merton's *No Man Is An Island*. (See page 20 for the quote as we read it that day.) Buying Merton's book for my friend, that night I became an eager reader, and had to buy another copy for my buddy. This writing of Trappist monk Thomas Merton began an adult conversion that has made for me all the difference.

Here are Thomas Merton's unedited words from *No Man Is An Island* [(1955, pg. 168)]:

He alone holds the secret of a charity
by which we can love others
not only as we love ourselves, but as He loves them.
The beginning of this love is
the will to let those we love be perfectly themselves,
the resolution not to twist them to fit our own image.

If in loving them we do not love what they are,
but only their potential likeness to ourselves,
then we do not love them: we only love
the reflection of ourselves we find in them.
Can this be charity?

It may have been a mistake for me to share this quote with a teenager's mother, who gave me what one old friend calls "the ugly mother look." She admitted that there was some truth to what Merton was saying, but was still challenged with her vocation as parent. I found myself cheering her on. But a grown-up addict is not the same thing as a mother's own still-growing child. When a mother of a grown-up addict gives me the ugly mother response to Merton's wisdom, we usually find more to talk about. The pattern of the enabler is a very difficult one to break.

What does Merton's wisdom have to do with the 8th and 9th Steps? It tells me that people we love are people we harm. Naming the people I have hurt, a willingness to make amends to them, and making amends whenever possible is part of the journey for every Christian, for every human person trying to live a good life.

The central thought is **willingness** - to admit our errors so we can clear our inner consciousness of guilt.

The only action this [the 8th] Step calls for is to **make a list**. I can do this by allowing my oppressive, nagging guilts to rise to the surface of my mind, ready to be disposed of, so they can trouble me no more.

"The 8th Step places us on the threshold of freedom from self-hate; it opens the door to new peace of mind, which, once enjoyed, we will never want to lose." (One Day At A Time in Al-Anon, 2000, June 22, pg. 174)

People who have been hurt by others will sometimes name that hurt as the cause of everything that has gone wrong in their life. To realize that we have also hurt others can be a great shock, and slogans (*Welcome to the human race!*) or the kind of cheerleading that permits us to escalate our feelings of hurt might make us feel better in the moment, but fall short of the healing that can come from holy honesty. We share a deep human desire for the kind of friend with whom we can vent without the need for consolation, challenge, or a fix. At times it is enough to simply be heard. Sometimes we need a good kick.

One cogent lesson from being a parish priest has been the idea that each of us carries some kind of core wound, usually but not always from our early years. This is one way to see the call of Jesus to pick up our cross daily and follow after him. God touches this wound at different times, sometimes asking us to allow a more deep level of healing. Whenever we convince ourselves that we have been completely healed of this core wound, it will soon confront us again.

As real as the core wound is, it does not take away my personal responsibility for what I do. The Christian examination of conscience is sterile if I think my faults are disconnected from the other people in my life. In holy honesty, can I name the people that I know that I have hurt? In holy honesty, can I trust that even when I have hurt another, God did not stop loving me? In holy honesty, can I discern that not every instance was a freely chosen sin? In holy honesty, can I also be aware that someone else thinking that I have hurt them does not make it so? Often the witness of another gives the best guidance:

> In my case, …the problem was…in letting go of my exaggerated sense of responsibility… Other people's expectations are not my responsibility unless I have helped to create them. I can remind myself that conflict is part of life.
> (Courage To Change, April 10, pg. 101)

Asking forgiveness, in a sense, is really a survival tactic. Many of the wrongs I did to other people were done out of resentment for who the other person was, or what they had that I didn't. We know from the program that holding onto resentments is one of the quickest ways of getting back into active using. Resentments foment and boil within us. They consume our every waking moment, and oftentimes even find ways into our dreams at night. We can only continue on our road to recovery by letting go of those past hurts, by confronting them straight on, and by seeking to make amends wherever humanly possible. We do this with only one caution: *that making the amends causes no further injury.* (Behnke, day 12)

The thought of my homeless poverty
is wormwood and gall;
remembering it over and over
leaves my soul downcast within me.
But I will call this to mind, as my reason to hope:
the favors of the Lord are not exhausted,
his mercies are not spent;
they are renewed each morning,
so great is his faithfulness.
My portion is the Lord, says my soul;
therefore will I hope in him.

Lamentations 3:19-24

a meditation

Imagine a world where forgiveness is impossible;
a world where everyone has to be perfect
in order to be loved.
Imagine a world where no one would love you
if you made even one mistake,
where no one ever got a chance
to make up for what they did wrong.
Imagine a world where each person was allowed only
one mistake, and once they used it up,
they could never be forgiven again.
Imagine a world where the first argument between
friends meant that the relationship was over,
and it could never be restored.
Imagine a world where parents had to stop loving
their kids the first time they
disobeyed or broke a rule.
Imagine a world where teachers would give up on
their students the first time they misbehaved.
Imagine a world where you could never admit a
mistake, or tell someone you're sorry, or
nobody could ever tell you they're sorry,
because forgiveness was impossible.
A world like that can only be imagined
– because it doesn't exist.

James Penrice, *You Know More Than You Think,* Alba House, 2003, pg. 35

an exercise for eight & nine

A - List five people (by initial only) whom you have hurt or who have hurt you. Circle those who are most important in your life. Pick one of them, and tell God how you feel about him or her (guilty, afraid, estranged).

B - Make an effort, with God's help, to understand why the situation happened. (Were either of you immature or hurting? What needs were you trying to meet? Toward whom were you harboring resentment?)

C - Make an agreement with yourself and God to make amends with this person if at all possible, perhaps by writing a letter, talking with him or her, or turning it over to God. Write down your agreement.

D - Consider whether you have a felt need to go to the sacrament of reconciliation.

E - Through prayer and meditation, look for some good that has come from your endeavor to be reconciled with the person you hurt or who hurt you (maturity, wisdom, service…). Write down what happened and the good that resulted.

F - Rinse and repeat.

from Vernon J. Bittner's *You Can Help With Your Healing*

51

one more caution

I have met people who have so dramatically harmed other people, even loved ones, that the only way to make amends is to live the remainder of one's years in as good a way as possible, seeking to do no more harm. Perfection is impossible; all any of us can do is to stay open to the gift of grace.

I know addicts who stay in the program, knowing that they may not be reconciled with family members in this life, but as the best amends they can still offer: the awareness that, today anyway, an estranged loved one is sober, meaning that no one else is being hurt today. When those are the only amends that do no harm, it can still bring a taste of peace at the end of the day.

REFLECTION

*from Vernon J. Bittner's *You Can Help With Your Healing*

1. Our Lord has promised to forgive us. Why is it that sometimes we do not have serenity?

2.* In the Lord's Prayer we say "forgive us...as we forgive..." What do these words mean in my life?

3. "Sin" means something is (a) wrong, (b) I know it's wrong, **and** (c) I freely do it. So, how could something do harm, and yet not be a sin?

4. "Restitution" means to make things right, to restore the situation, when it is possible and won't make things worse. When it is not possible to make amends, what then can we do?

5.* Many illnesses are a result of unresolved stress. How has my physical body suffered from stress and other problems?

6. Have I ever experienced a time of healing of painful memories?

7. Can I name a time of healing that came from a change in attitude about a person or a situation?

Closing Prayer: Are there intercessions from the group?

Conclude with the Our Father, then the prayer and song on pages 74 and 75.

Tenth Step Prayer

I pray I may continue:
to grow in understanding and effectiveness;
to take daily spot check inventories of myself;
to correct mistakes when I make them;
to take responsibility for my actions; to be ever aware
　　　of my negative and self-defeating attitudes and behaviors;
to keep my willfulness in check;
to always remember I need your help;
to keep love and tolerance of others as my code;
and to continue in daily prayer how I can best serve you,
my Higher Power.

Eleventh Step Prayer

Higher Power, as I understand you, I pray to keep my
connection with you open and clear from the confusion of daily life.
Through my prayers and meditations I will ask especially
for freedom from self-will, rationalization, and wishful thinking.
I pray for the guidance of correct thought and positive action.
Your will, Higher Power, not mine, be done.

Twelfth Step Prayer

Dear God, my spiritual awakening continues to unfold.
The help I have received I shall pass on and give to others,
both in and out of the Fellowship. For this opportunity I am grateful.
I pray most humbly to continue walking day by day on the road of
spiritual progress. I pray for the inner strength and wisdom
to practice the principles of this way of life in all I do and say.
I need you, my friends, and the Program every hour of every day.
This is a better way to live.

The Twelve Step Prayer Book, page 70, 71

6

One Day At A Time

10th step We continue to take personal inventory, and when we are wrong, promptly admit it, and when we are right, thank God for the guidance.
(Bittner)

11th step We seek through prayer and meditation to improve our conscious contact with Jesus Christ as we understand him, praying for the knowledge of his will for us and the power to carry that out.
(Bittner)

12th step Having experienced a new sense of spirituality as a result of these steps, and realizing that this is a gift of God's grace, we are willing to share the message of God's love and forgiveness with others, and practice these principles for [incarnational] living in all our affairs.
(Bittner)

55

One member of the group reads: **Philippians 2:5-11**
as other members read silently.

2nd member of the group reads: **Romans 10:14-17**
as other members read silently.

3rd member of the group reads: **Matthew 18:10-14**
as other members read silently.

Take turns reading the following background reflections from Addiction and Grace, by Gerald G. May, M.D. (Harper & Row, 1988) and from "Pass It On:"The Story of BillWilson and How the A.A. Message Reached theWorld (A.A., 1984).

Jesus is led into the desert by the Holy Spirit. Hungry and vulnerable, he is tempted. He responds out of his own freedom and faith, and he is protected by angels. Satan is then defeated, temporarily, and Jesus comes forth for his ministry.

Jesus was tempted to fall prey to attachment: attachment to meeting his own needs, attachment to his own power, or attachment to the material riches of the world, the "I can handle it" trap.

It is easy to ascribe Jesus' success in the desert to who he was: the chosen one, God incarnate. Seeing him in such magnificence can make it difficult for us to identify with him. But if we think of Jesus as truly human [,fully divine and fully human], as a real man who was vulnerable to the attachment, then the way he responded to Satan's temptations reveals something. Jesus' actions in the wilderness reveal the way through all our deserts, the way home.

First, Jesus stood firm. He met the adversary, faced the temptation, and did not run away or rationalize. He met the challenge as it was. Second, he acted with strength: he claimed and used his free will with dignity. Third, and most important for our culture, **he did not use his freedom willfully**. None of his responses to Satan was his own autonomous creation. Instead, he relied on the Law: quotations from Scripture, from the Torah. Herein lies the practical key to the mystery of human and divine will, the essence of dealing with addiction.

Addiction cannot be defeated by the human will acting on its own, nor by the human will opting out and turning everything over to divine will. Instead, *the power of grace flows most fully when human will chooses to act in harmony with divine will.* In practical terms, this means staying in a situation, being willing to confront it as it is, remaining responsible for the choices one makes in response to it, but at the same time turning to God's grace, protection, and guidance as the ground for one's choices and behavior. It is the difference between *testing* God by avoiding one's own responsibilities and *trusting* God as one acts responsibly. Responsible human freedom thus becomes authentic spiritual surrender, and authentic spiritual surrender is nothing other than

responsible human freedom. Here, in the condition of humble dignity, the power of addiction can be overcome.
(Gerald May, *Addiction and Grace*, pgs. 137-139)

Every sincere battle with addiction begins with an attempt to change addictive behavior. Literally, we try to *reform our behavior.* Reformation of behavior usually involves *substituting* one addiction for another new, possibly less destructive normality. Sometimes substitution is intentional, sometimes unconscious. An overeater adapts to jogging and yoga; a smoker adapts to chewing gum or eating; a television addict becomes dependent upon guided meditations; an aggressive person becomes accustomed to ingratiating behavior; an alcoholic becomes addicted to A.A. This way of fighting addiction is like weaning; it is an attempt to make the transition to independence as painless as possible. Sometimes it works; often it does not.

Substitution allows us to avoid the open, empty feeling that comes when an addictive behavior is curtailed. Although this emptiness is really freedom, it is so unconditional that it feels strange, sometimes even horrible. If we were willing for a deeper transformation of desire, we would have to try to make friends with spaciousness, to appreciate it as openness to God.

Because openness to God is threatening, and because our desire is more to overcome an addiction than to claim our deeper desire for God, we fill the space for something else. In so doing, we assent to continued slavery under a new master who, we hope, will be kinder. But if the new normality is indeed kinder, it will almost surely seem insufficient. There is also no guarantee that our new master will be kinder than the old.

When reformation "works," it is well worth it. It may even be life saving. We will have had the experience of the struggle, and we will have learned something about ourselves. It may allow us to step further into the next desert. We may be that much closer to making friends with spaciousness, to recognizing God's inevitable homeward call, the invitation to the transformation of our desire.

Every struggle with addiction, no matter how small, and no matter what our spiritual interest may be, will include at least brief encounters with spaciousness. Through the spaciousness will come some homeward call, some invitation to transformation. If we answer yes, even with the tiniest and most timid voice, our struggle becomes *consecrated*. **Consecration** means dedication to God. It occurs when we claim our deepest desire for God, beneath, above, and beyond all things. In consecration we dedicate our struggle to something more than minimizing the pain that addiction causes us and others; consecration is our assent to God's transforming grace, our commitment homeward.

In the beginning we will not understand the full meaning of consecration. Perhaps, in this life, we never will. But our yes comes from some taste, some bare

59

recollection of encountering spaciousness. We feel a small breeze of freedom. And in the tiny space our hearts can say yes.

Consider an absurd question:

If I say yes to God, if I do consecrate myself,
will that help me to overcome my addiction?

Why absurd?   Because it contains an impossible contradiction. If I am primarily dedicated to overcoming addiction, I cannot really be consecrated [primarily] to God. ^(Gerald May, *Addiction and Grace*, pgs. 146-151)

Gerald May, MD, psychiatrist, shares many stories of the working of unpredictable grace. One recovering alcoholic said,

Grace, mediated by a fair amount of humiliation,
has lightened me up a bit.

It happened to a middle-aged steelworker while he was going to the market; he said later,

I didn't fight the desire to drink anymore;
I just didn't drink.

A middle-aged lawyer who was addicted to sex suddenly was able to say to his lover,

This is the last time I'll be here.

She must have read something on his face when she responded,   *I know.*

A woman who was addicted to stress said one day,

I quit. I don't even know what I quit. I just quit.

Over time, as she just did the next thing she needed to do, she slowed down. (May, from pgs. 152-159)

In the first week of Ordinary Time, the five or six days following the Feast of the Baptism of the Lord, Catholic liturgy uses this opening prayer:

Father of love, hear our prayers.
Help us to know your will
and to do it with courage and faith.

A few months before noted psychiatrist Carl Jung died in 1961, he wrote this in a short exchange of letters with Bill W.:

I am strongly convinced that the evil principle prevailing in this world leads the unrecognized spiritual need into a perdition, if it is not counteracted either by a real religious insight or by the protective wall of human community. An ordinary person, not protected by an action from above and isolated in society, cannot resist the process of evil... Alcohol in latin is **spiritus,** *and you use the same word for the highest religious experience as well as for the most depraving poison. The helpful formula therefore is:* **spiritus contra spiritum.** ("Pass It On," page 384)

61

In the great book telling the story of A.A., *"Pass It On,"* there are crossroads from the early days when they were trying to find their way. It is a story of collaboration and listening. Bill W. was asked at one point to do this work as a "job." The pressures were strong; he had a family to support. However, he followed the strong advice of those in the fellowship, and a fellowship it remained.

And so, like all the traditions by which any person or group lives, these evolved as this growing group of people responded to what happens in the middle of growing.

The results strike many as an impressive collection of simple wisdom for any organization that might dare to trust completely in God.   - Stephen Joseph Wolf

The Twelve Traditions of A.A.

1. Our common welfare should come first; personal recovery depends upon A.A. unity.

2. For our group purpose there is but one ultimate authority - a loving God as He may express Himself in our group conscience. Our leaders are but trusted servants; they do not govern.

3. The only requirement for A.A. membership is a desire to stop drinking.

4. Each group should be autonomous except in matters affecting other groups or A.A. as a whole.

5. Each group has but one primary purpose - to carry its message to the alcoholic who still suffers.

6. An A.A. group ought never endorse, finance, or lend the A.A. name to any related facility or outside enterprise, lest problems of money, property, and prestige divert us from our primary purpose.

7. Every A.A. group ought to be fully self-supporting, declining outside contributions.

8. Alcoholics Anonymous should remain forever non-professional, but our service centers may employ social workers.

9. A.A., as such, ought never be organized; but we may create service boards or committees directly responsible to those they serve.

10. Alcoholics Anonymous has no opinion on outside issues; hence the A.A. name ought never be drawn into public controversy.

11. Our public relations policy is based on attraction rather than promotion; we need always maintain personal anonymity at the level of press, radio and films.

12. Anonymity is the spiritual foundation of all our traditions, ever reminding us to place principles above personalities.

The Twelve Steps of A.A.

1. We admitted we were powerless over alcohol, that our lives had become unmanageable.

2. Came to believe that a Power greater than ourselves could restore us to sanity.

3. Made a decision to turn our will and our lives over to the care of God *as we understood Him.*

4. Made a searching and fearless moral inventory of ourselves.

5. Admitted to God, to ourselves, and to another human being the exact nature of our wrongs.

6. Were entirely ready to have God remove all these defects of character.

7. Humbly asked Him to remove our shortcomings.

8. Made a list of all persons we had harmed, and became willing to make amends to them all.

9. Made direct amends to such people wherever possible, except when to do so would injure them or others.

10. Continued to take personal inventory and when we were wrong promptly admitted it.

11. Sought through prayer and meditation to improve our conscious contact with God *as we understood Him* praying only for knowledge.

12. Having had a spiritual awakening as the result of these steps, we tried to carry this message to alcoholics, and to practice these principles in all our affairs.

REFLECTION

* from Vernon J. Bittner's *You Can Help With Your Healing*

1. Fr. Bill Fleming (d. 1999) used to conclude the general intercessions (prayer of the faithful) with this prayer: **Give us the grace to know your will; give us the courage to do it.** Is there another way I want to pray this?

2.* How do I sometimes frustrate my own efforts?

3. How do I feel about the word "consecration"?

4.* What is the purpose of prayer?

5.* Why does it seem difficult at times to set aside a period of time each day for prayer and meditation? What can I do to make this happen?

6.* How do I celebrate my growth in Christ?

7.* How might the format of working with these twelve steps in my daily life help me give witness to others about my faith journey?

8. How might I continue this process?

9.* What is the best way for me to share the message of love and forgiveness, the message of salvation through Christ, with others?

Closing Prayer: Are there intercessions from the group?

Conclude with the Our Father, then the prayer and song on pages 74 and 75.

Attraction Addictions

anger
approval
art
attractiveness
being good
being helpful
being loved
being nice
being normal
being right
being taken care of
calendars
candy
cars
causes
chewing gum
children
chocolate
cleanliness
coffee
comparisons
competence
competition
computers
contests
death
depression
dreams
drinking
drugs
eating
envy
exercise
fame
family
fantasies

finger drumming
fishing
food
friends
furniture
gambling
gardening
golf
gossiping
groups
guilt
hair twisting
happiness
hobbies
housekeeping
humor
hunting
ice cream
images of God
intimacy
jealousy
knowledge
lying
marriage
meeting expectations
memories
messiness
money
movies
music
nail biting
neatness
parents
performance
pets

pimple squeezing
pistachio nuts
pizza
politics
popcorn
popularity
potato chips
power
psychotherapy
punctuality
reading
relationships
responsibility
revenge
scab picking
seductiveness
self-image
self-improvement
sex
shoplifting
sleeping
soft drinks
sports
status
stock market
stress
sunbathing
suspiciousness
talking
television
time
tobacco
weight
winning
work
worthiness

Aversion Addictions

airplanes
anchovies
anger
animals
being:
   abnormal
   alone
   discounted
   fat
   judged
   overwhelmed
   thin
   tricked
birds
blood
boredom
bridges
bugs
cats
closed-in spaces
commitment
conflict
crowds
darkness
death
dentists

dependence
dirt
disapproval
doctors
embarrassment
evil spirits
failure
fire
germs
guilt
high places
illness
independence
intimacy
mice
needles
open spaces
pain
people of different:
   beliefs
   class
   culture
   politics
   race
   religion
   sex

people who are:
   addicted
   competent
   fat / thin
   ignorant
   neat / messy
   rich / poor
public speaking
rats
rejection
responsibility
sex
sharp instruments
slimy creatures
snakes
spiders
storms
strangers
success
tests
traffic
tunnels
vulnerability
water
writing

No addiction is good; no attachment is beneficial. To be sure, some are more destructive than others; alcoholism cannot be compared with chocolate addiction in degrees of destructiveness, and fear of spiders pales in comparison to racial bigotry. But if we accept that there are differences in the degree of tragedy imposed on us by our addictions, we must also recognize what they have in common: they impede human freedom and diminish the human spirit.

From *Addiction and Grace,* Gerald G. May, M.D., 1988, pages 38-39

Just for Today

Just for today I will try to live through this day only, and not tackle my whole life problem at once. I can do something for twelve hours that would appall me if I felt that I had to keep it up for a lifetime.

Just for today I will be happy. This assumes to be true what Abraham Lincoln said, that "Most folks are as happy as they make up their minds to be."

Just for today I will adjust myself to what is, and not try to adjust everything else to my own desires. I will take my "luck" as it comes, and fit myself to it.

Just for today I will try to strengthen my mind. I will study; I will learn something useful; I will not be a mental loafer; I will read something that requires effort, thought and concentration.

Just for today I will exercise my soul in three ways: I will do somebody a good turn, and not get found out; if anybody knows of it, it will not count; I will do at least two things I don't want to do - just for exercise. I will not show anyone that my feelings are hurt; they may be hurt, but today I will not show it.

Just for today I will be agreeable. I will look as good as I can, dress becomingly, talk low, act courteously, criticize not one bit, not find fault with anything, and not try to improve or regulate anybody except myself.

Just for today I will have a program. I may not follow it exactly, but I will have it. I will save myself from two pests: hurry and indecision.

Just for today I will have a quiet half hour all by myself, and relax. During this half hour, sometime, I will try to get a better perspective on my life.

Just for today I will be unafraid. I will enjoy that which is beautiful, and will believe that as I give to the world, so the world will give to me.

From *The Twelve Step Prayer Book,* Glen Abbey Books, 1990, page 79

Twelve Steps For Christian Living
Vernon J. Bittner, 1979

1. We admit our need for God's gift of salvation, that we are powerless over certain areas of our lives and that our lives are at times sinful and unmanageable.

2. We come to believe through the Holy Spirit that a power who came in the person of Jesus Christ and who is greater than ourselves can transform our weaknesses into strengths.

3. We make a decision to turn our will and our lives over to the care of Christ as we understand him—hoping to understand him more fully.

4. We make a searching and fearless moral inventory of ourselves—both our strengths and our weaknesses.

5. We admit to Christ, to ourselves, and to another human being the exact nature of our sins.

6. We become entirely ready to have Christ heal all of these defects of character that prevent us from having a more spiritual life-style.

7. We humbly ask Christ to transform all of our shortcomings.

8. We make a list of all persons we have harmed and become willing to make amends to them all.

9. We make direct amends to such persons whenever possible, except when to do so would injure them or others.

10. We continue to take personal inventory, and when we are wrong, promptly admit it, and when we are right, thank God for the guidance.

11. We seek through prayer and meditation to improve our conscious contact with Jesus Christ as we understand him, praying for the knowledge of his will for us and the power to carry that out.

12. Having experienced a new sense of spirituality as a result of these steps and realizing that this is a gift of God's grace, we are willing to share the message of God's love and forgiveness with others and practice these principles for spiritual living in all our affairs.

See also
Twelve Steps For Christian Living: Growth in a New Way of Living
by Vernon J. Bittner, 1987

Sources & For More

You Can Help With Your Healing: A Guide for Recovering Wholeness in Body, Mind, and Spirit, Vernon J. Bittner, Augsburg, 1993, 12 chapters including a Study Guide,155 pages; a bestseller outstanding for groups or individuals going deeper with the steps one at a time; beginning on pages 7, 13, 18, 23, 33, 43, 51, 55 and 70. Used with permission

90 Days, One Day At A Time: A New Beginning for People in Recovery, John Behnke, C.S.P., Paulist Press, Inc., 1999, 158 pages, a great resource for 90 days; beginning on pages 8, 14, 24, 34 and 48. Used with permission.

Addiction and Grace, Gerald G. May, M.D., Harper & Row, San Francisco, 1988, 8 chapters, 200 pages, a modern classic?; beginning on pages 56, 58, 60 and 66. Used with permission.

*Al-Anon's Twelve Steps & Twelve Traditions, Al-Anon Family Group Headquarters, Inc., 1981, 2005, 150 pages; see page 44.

*Courage to Change: One Day At A Time In Al-Anon II, Al-Anon Group Headquarters, Inc., 1992, 380 pages; see page 48.

*One Day At A Time In Al-Anon, Al-Anon Family Group Headquarters, Inc., 1985, 367 pages; see page 20.

*One Day At A Time In Al-Anon, Al-Anon Family Group Headquarters, Inc., 2000, 378 pages; see pages 10, 47.

No Man Is An Island, Thomas Merton, 1955, page 168; see pages 20 and 46.

"Pass It On:" The Story of Bill Wilson and How the A.A. Message Reached the World, A.A., 1984, 429 pages, part of American history; see pages 5, 61 and 62.

Saint Meinrad Prayer Book, Saint Meinrad Alumni
Association, Abbey Press, 1995, 188 pages; _{beginning on page 27.}

*The Spirituality of Imperfectiion: Storytelling and
the Journey to Wholeness,* Ernest Kurtz and
Kathleen Ketcham, Bantam Books, 1992, 16 chapters,
294 pages.

Theological Reflection: Connecting Faith and Life,
Joye Gros, O.P., Loyola Press, 2002; see page *iv.*

*Twelve Steps to Spiritual Wholeness: A Christian
Pathway,* Philip St. Romain, Liguori Publications,
1992, 12 chapters with Questions for Reflection, 96 pages.

The Twelve Step Prayer Book, written and compiled by
Bill Pittman, Glen Abbey Books, 1990, 111 pages; see pages 6,
12, 22, 32, 42, 54, 68 and 69.

*You Know More Than You Think: Your Intuitive
Knowledge of God in the Catholic Tradition,*
James Penrice, Alba House, 2003, 18 chapters, 124 pages;
see page 50. Used with permission.

Will and Spirit, Gerald G. May, M.D., Harper San
Francisco, 1982, 11 chapters, 360 pages; see page 3.
Used with permission.

CLOSING PRAYER

God, grant me the serenity
to accept the things I cannot change,
courage to change the things I can,
and wisdom to know the difference.
Living one day at a time,
enjoying one moment at a time,
accepting hardships as a pathway to peace,
taking as Jesus did,
this sinful world as it is,
not as I would have it,
trusting that you will make all things right
if I surrender to your will,
so that I may be
reasonably happy in this life
and supremely happy with you
forever in the next.
Amen.

CLOSING SONG

Amazing Grace!   How sweet the sound
That saved a wretch like me.
I once was lost, but now am found,
Was blind, but now I see.

'**Twas** grace that taught my heart to fear,
And grace my fears relieved.
How precious did that grace appear
The hour I first believed.

Through many dangers, toils, and snares,
I have already come.
'Tis grace hath brought me safe thus far,
And grace will lead me home.

When we've been there ten thousand years,
Bright shining as the sun,
We've no less days to sing God's praise
Than when we'd first begun.

John Newton, 1779

LaVergne, TN USA
25 August 2010
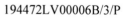
194472LV00006B/3/P